The Lumina Chronicles

A Fantasy Coloring Experience

by Cristina McAllister

The Lumina Chronicles; A Fantasy Coloring Experience

Edited by Dee Fromson
Made possible by Team 1 1/2 ❤

Dedicated to the writers and artists who have created worlds of imagination and invited me to
explore.

Published by Gypsy Mystery Arts
http://www.GypsyMystery.com

Printed by CreateSpace

ISBN-13: 978-1523739462

ISBN-10: 1523739460

Introduction

This book is a little different from your average coloring book.

To get the full experience, I recommend reading through the entire book, including the information at the back, before diving into coloring. By then, you should have plenty of inspiration to fuel your creativity.

The writings and images in this book are excerpts from the contents of a very peculiar antique folio that came into my possession several years ago. I am a collector of interesting old books, especially illustrated books. My budget is modest, but on occasion I will come across a rare treasure in a thrift store, a hole-in-the-wall bookshop, or through a friend.

The folio, which had passed through several private collections and estate sales, contains two bound notebooks, as well as numerous loose sheets filled with hand-written notes, sketches and calculations. There are also over two dozen "Luminographs" (extraordinary images created with a unique photographic process). The original prints had faded and darkened over time, so I scanned and digitally enhanced them for clarity.

The provenance of these papers is mysterious, and their content is astonishing and fascinating. My attempts to find more information about it have proved mostly fruitless.

The author is listed as J.M. Smythe, a name so common that it is nearly impossible to identify pertinent records.

Though there are no dates mentioned, the events described within (if they really happened) seem to have taken place during the mid-to-late 1800's, during the Victorian era. Archival analysis of the bindings, paper, ink and language support this.

From context clues, I suspect the location to be somewhere in the English countryside within a day's travel to London.

We will probably never know if this fantastical collection is a factual account, the ravings of a madman or a hoax. In any case, it is a fascinating glimpse into another time and another world.

The burgeoning science of light and optics is one of great fascination for me, being both a scholar of Natural Philosophy and an artist. I have painted since my youth, and I am not so humble as to deny that I have some legitimate, natural talent. From the beginning, how to place the colors upon the canvas was an intuitive adventure that I persued with gusto. What my eye can see, I can translate into imagery with innate ease. Even the pictures in my mind I can accurately portray, though they may be pure fantasy.

Often I am compelled to forgo any semblance of Realism and simply splash the colors about the canvas with abandon. Though they may seem to be cacophonous jumbles of nonsensical chaos, and I would certainly never display them in public (I would likely be ridiculed at best - at worst, thrown into "The Retreat" with the lunatics) - for me, the process itself is one of purest bliss.

Colors (and therefor Light) are a part of my being, and I am infinitely curious about their secrets, so I have endeavored to follow in the footsteps of such literal luminaries as Newton, Goethe and Brewster and explore the matter myself.

One thing that sparked my interest was the refractionary properties of crystals. I had heard tales that the ancient Vikings made use of "sunstones", polarizing crystals that helped them to locate the sun on cloudy days in order to navigate their frigid seas.
It is speculated that a crystalline mineral known as Iceland Spar is the stone in question, and I was quite keen on acquiring a specimen.

Unfortunately, such stones are rare and difficult to come by, and I exhausted every avenue of legitimate inquiry with no results. I am afraid I was even compelled, in my desperation, to approach some rather unsavory characters with reputations for producing rare items through dubious means.

Special Effect: Aged Parchment

Begin with a soft layer of yellowish - cream or tan over the entire area.

Using a reddish brown, delicately tint the darker areas around the edges. Build this up in light layers, striving for an irregular, mottled pattern.

Continue to add sheer patches of different shades of brown, warm gray and golden yellow until the page looks sufficiently aged.

Viking "Sunstone"

Iceland Spar
Crystal

The Dragons' teeth
would serve as prongs to
hold the crystal in place.

There are a number of
examples of Viking torcs
and pendants with gaps between
decorative endcaps. They are
assumed to be merely
adornments, but what if some
were used as navigational
instruments?

A suitable piece of Iceland
Spar crystal would be mounted
within the device, which would serve
as a handle to hold it up to the
overcast sky and search for the sun's
glow through the crystal's polarizing
matrix. Here I have imagined
such a device, as might have been
crafted by a master
metalsmith of the
Viking Age.

Embellished with
decorative inlays of
colorful enamel and
precious stones.

"Thor's Hammer"
motif

Some months after giving up this quest and moving on to other enterprises, a mysterious package arrived at my door.

Its origins were not evident — no sender's name or address, not even a postmark. It was a simple paper-wrapped parcel tied securely with twine.

Underneath several layers of oakum padding was a small cardboard box such as one would package cigars or pastilles in, adorned with colorful decorative flourishes and an exotic-looking design upon the lid.

Inside, nestled in a velvet-lined depression, was a round crystal disc. It was about a half of an inch thick, and four inches across.

At first I thought it to be some sort of lens, such as those used in microscopes and other optical devices, but the top and bottom surfaces were not in any way artificially shaped. They were mostly flat, with the natural irregularities of a raw crystal.

The stone was colorless, and somewhat cloudy...yet as I held it and turned it this way and that in the light, I could see prismatic flashes of color within.

I am unable to identify the style of this motif, which adorns the box the crystal arrived in.

The spiral roundels within the marquis shapes resemble mesmer—izing eyes.

Dea

I

crystal

It is

Icelan

I requ

quality a

prepared

Please

The rich colors ren

stained glass or

illuminat

of

I am unable to identify the style of this motif, which adorns the box the crystal arrived in.

The spiral roundels within the marquis shapes resemble mesmerizing eyes.

The rich colors remind me of stained glass or the colorful illuminated manuscripts of the *Middle Ages*.

As I sit down to sketch out this design, it seems to me that the colors are different from when I first inspected the box. I recall admiring specific shades and wondering what pigments were used. Now those shades are entirely different, as if the colors have shifted. Is that possible…?

Spirals are one of the oldest symbols used by *Man*, and often symbolise magic or mystical energy.

Book 1

Opticks:
Or, A Treastise
of the
Reflections,
Refractions,
Inflexions
and Colors
of Light

A Treatise on Optics

by

Sir David Brewster, LL.D., F.R.S.

Part II

Isaac Newton

At first, I assumed that this was the sample of Iceland Spar I had been seeking, though its rounded shape was most unusual and not precisely what I had requested. More perplexing, though, was that none of my acquisition contacts claimed to know anything about it. How it found its way to me is a mystery that haunts me to this day.

But it soon became apparent to me that the crystal was not, in fact, Iceland Spar. Instead of the characteristic polarizing, double-refraction effect, this crystal possessed prismatic qualities that produced vague patterns of spectral colors, quite unlike anything I'd seen before.

The raw, filmy surface made clear observations of these curious effects impossible, even under the microscope. So I set about polishing the stone, and after several applications of abrasive paste and a generous helping of elbow grease, the strange disc's hazy sheen was transformed. The surfaces were now almost perfectly clear, gleaming and glass-like.

The colorful patterns within could be discerned with much better clarity now, but I could not help feeling disappointment at my observations. The flashes of light appeared as ephemeral beams that seemed to bounce around within the crystal in a random, tangled mess.

Something about their chaotic arrangement bothered me, and I was seized with the notion to continue with my lapidarian modifications in order to perfect the stone and enhance its chromatic attributes.

Special Effect: Crystal Clear

Try coloring the wallpaper pattern in rich colors, but leave the crystal white, with perhaps whispers of gray or light blue. Add shimmering smudges of many different colors in the crystal's center.

Try adding some extra sparkle with a clear glitter gel pen.

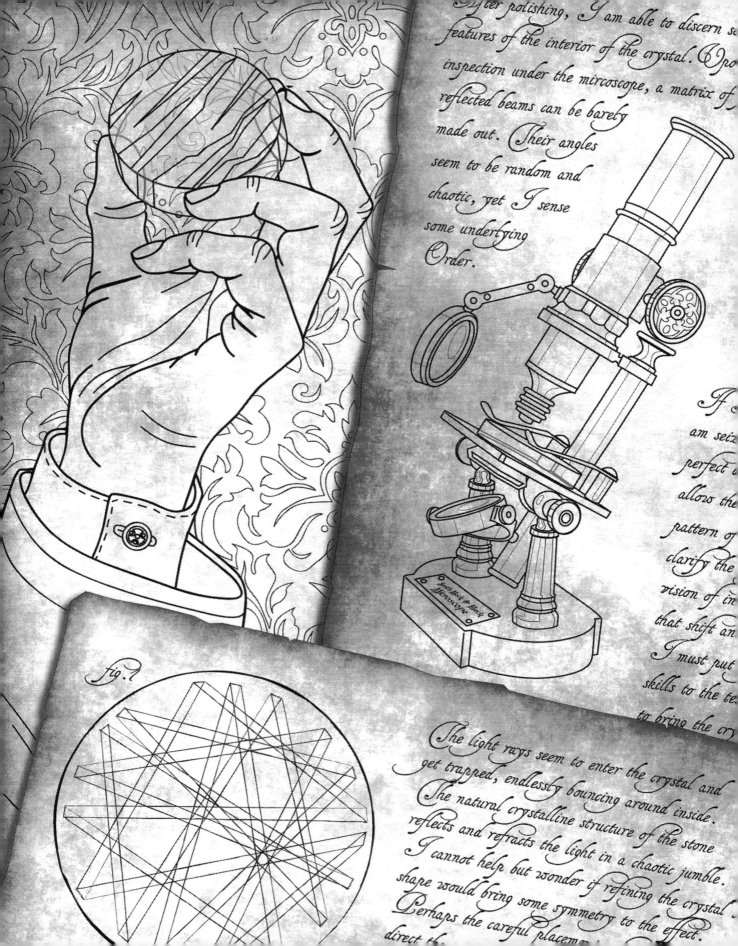

features of the interior of the crystal. Upo...
inspection under the mircoscope, a matrix of
reflected beams can be barely
made out. Their angles
seem to be random and
chaotic, yet I sense
some underlying
Order.

I ...
am seiz...
perfect ...
allow the...
pattern of ...
clarify the ...
vision of in...
that shift an...
I must put ...
skills to the te...
to bring the cry...

Smith Bock & Buck Microscope

fig. 1

The light rays seem to enter the crystal and
get trapped, endlessly bouncing around inside.
The natural crystalline structure of the stone
reflects and refracts the light in a chaotic jumble.
I cannot help but wonder if refining the crystal
shape would bring some symmetry to the effect.
Perhaps the careful placeme...
direct th...

I was already familiar with the basic principles of lens grinding and gem cutting, but for this endeavor I felt I needed to expand my skills. I would only have one chance to cut this singular stone, and the thought of ruining it filled me with trepidation.

So I refreshed and developed my lapidary proficiency; researching various facet patterns, calculating angles of reflection and refraction and advancing my gemstone cutting techniques.

So enthralled was I with this endeavor that I even dreamt of glittering crystals, delicately sculpted into geometrical arrangements of flat planes that bent the light like a stately hall of mirrors, bouncing it around within the crystal in beautifully harmonious patterns. These dream images were often supernaturally vivid, and surprisingly, the sketches I fervently scribbled upon waking often produced very useful and relevant insights.

It took me two months of research, observation, analysis, experimentation and calculation to finalize the facet pattern that I hoped would bring the crystal's visions into focus.

I then spent another several weeks practicing my gem cutting skills. I went through almost two hundred low-grade crystals in my quest to master the techniques.

Fortunately, most of the resulting gems were quite lovely, and I was able to sell the lot to a canny jeweler in Hatton Gardens, who (undoubtedly) set them in gold and sold them to unsuspecting dandies as fine jewels.

In any case, once I was satisfied with the facet pattern and felt confident of my skills, I gathered the courage to make the fateful cuts.

Special Effect: Analogous Blend

Once you have filled in each colorspace with a single, flat color, try adding a blend of an Analogous color over half the colorspace.

Analogous colors are next to each other on the Color Wheel*.
For example: For a Yellow colorspace, blend in some Orange or Green.
For a Blue colorspace, blend in some Green or Violet.

Try blends at different angles - from the top down, from the bottom up, from one side, or at a diagonal.

*There is a Color Wheel included elsewhere in this book for you to refer to.

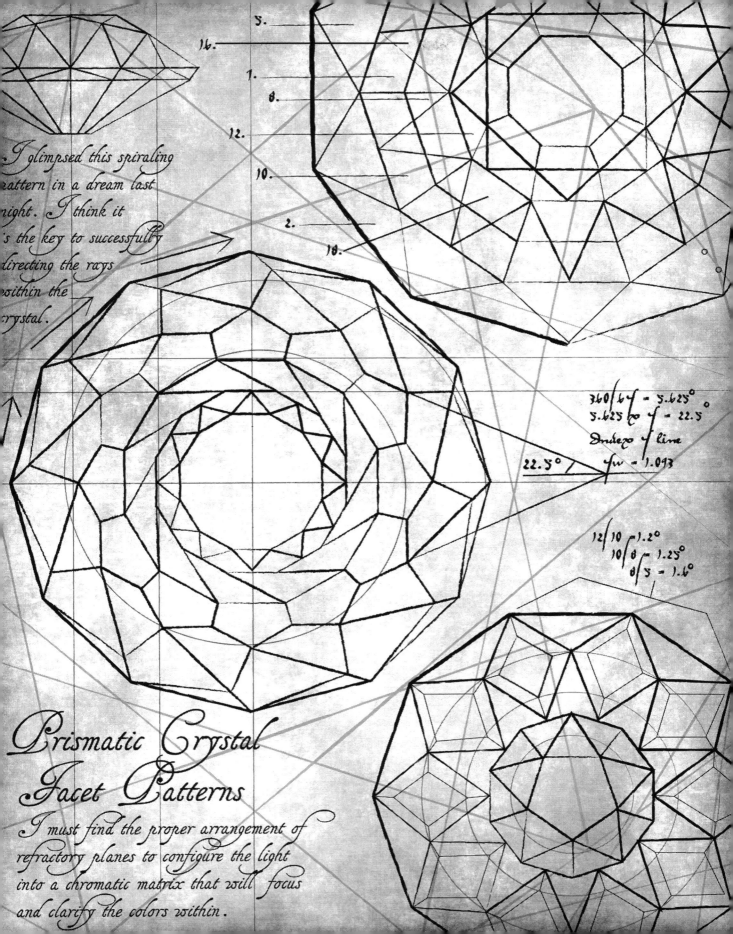

I glimpsed this spiraling
pattern in a dream last
night. I think it
is the key to successfully
directing the rays
within the
crystal.

5.
16.
1.
8.
12.
10.
2.
10.

$360/64 = 5.625°$
$5.625 \times 4 = 22.5$
Index of line
$t/w = 1.043$

$22.5°$

$12/10 = 1.2°$
$10/8 = 1.25°$
$8/5 = 1.6°$

Prismatic Crystal
Facet Patterns

I must find the proper arrangement of
refractory planes to configure the light
into a chromatic matrix that will focus
and clarify the colors within.

*I*ncredibly, I managed to sculpt the crystal with almost superhuman precision and skill. At times it felt as if some divine influence was guiding my hands. It was much like my abstract painting...an intuitive exercise in pursuing what felt RIGHT.

As I had hoped, the precise positioning of the facet planes now guided the rays of light around the crystal in a spiraling ring, leaving the central area clear, like a lens. Looking through this lens, the scenery around me was visible, but the colors were strangely altered — shimmering and shifting through the spectrum, and overlaying all, a faint tracery of geometric patterns that constantly moved and transformed.

At first, I thought my eyes must be fatigued, as I had been working long hours and engaged in intense concentration for weeks. The patterns were reminiscent of the "phosphenes" described by Savigny and Helmholz - those dazzling visions which dance behind the closed eyelids when pressure is applied, or when the mind is drifting between wakefulness and dreaming. They are thought to be figments of the optic nerve.

After a good night's sleep, I returned to my observations to find that the patterns were still visible through the crystal's gaze, though still exasperatingly vague and difficult to examine or describe. I spent many hours vainly chasing these ephemeral apparitions, trying to sketch out their forms, but the results were quite unsatisfactory.
Mrs. Gravely offered me a bottle of claret to sooth my agitated mind, and I confess, in my frustration, I downed several drams in quick succession, which had the "medicinal" effect of sending me forthwith to Dreamland. My inebriated mind conjured not soothing visions, but scenes of anxiety and failure — a nightmare of the Crystal Prism I had spent so much attention and effort upon shattering into a thousand pieces.

I started awake some hours later, in the depths of the night, slumped over my worktable. My lamps had gone out and all was in darkness. After a few moments of dismayed disorientation, I fumbled for the matches...but then something caught my eye.
A glimmer of light and color glowed in the darkness. It was the Crystal — alive with its own luminescence!

I reached for it and held it to my eye, and against the black field of night, the patterns came to life with such vividness and clarity that I cried out in astonishment. It was my "Eureka moment", though I'm afraid my utterance was less eloquent. I believe my exclamation of discovery was "Blimey..!", which is ironic considering the term is a minced oath of "blind me". Indeed, the opposite was the case — this accidental discovery has given me a new kind of vision I could never have imagined.

My eyes were dazzled with kaleidoscopic patterns that danced and pulsed with vibrant, ever-shifting colors. It was magnificent! My jaw dropped, my heart felt as if it would burst from my breast, and it seemed the very Music of the Spheres was somehow visually encoded in those brilliant, dancing patterns.

I hastily draped all the windows of my laboratory with some old mourning curtains to block out the intruding daylight. For two days, I sat in that darkened room, gazing through the Crystal at those mesmerizing vistas. I tried to sketch out what I saw to the best of my ability, but no static image could convey the dynamic dance of form and hue that swirled and pulsed before me.

What were these strange images? What was I seeing?

I quickly dismissed the notion of phosphenes or other phenomenon generated by my eyes or brain. The patterns were only apparent when I looked through the crystal, and as I swept my gaze around the room, the strange imagery remained fixed (though still constantly altering and transforming in both shape and color). It is difficult to describe this effect with words, but the veil of colors seemed to have dimension and depth – as if made of some matter that filled the space around me just as air surrounds us – invisible, but present nonetheless.

Was the Crystal revealing some new form of matter normally invisible to the human eye? Could I be seeing the elusive "Aetheric Medium" that Newton theorized was necessary for Light to propagate through space?

Obviously, Light and Color were involved, though not in any way I could recognize or understand. If this is the Luminiferous Aether thought to exist in the space around us, it is much more complex and mysterious than anyone had ever suspected!

The array of colors is staggering. Every hue and shade of the visible spectrum is present – and perhaps a few more. Sometimes I think I spy strange colors that I cannot quite identify and which defy all attempts to describe. Sometimes the color schemes are dark and dramatic, with rich jewel tones and flashes of gold or silver. Or they will burst into brilliant contrasting hues that seem to vibrate with saturated intensity. Other chromatic combinations are soft and harmonious – soothing symphonies of subtle shades that fade gracefully into each other.

Infinite spirals of vibrant colors, entwining, flowing, bubbling up like champagne effervescence…

At first, the shifting, morphing patterns seemed random to my ignorant mind, but after awhile, I sensed they were not simply chaos. There is an ineffable beauty and rhythm and intention flowing through them, a sense of infinite creativity and intelligence, as if they are being conjured by some Cosmic Artist - a consciousness beyond my comprehesion.

It is as if I am witnessing the very medium of Creation - the raw stuff of Reality being brought into being. Is this the mind of God? His primal palette of Genesis?

The notion is incredible - overwhelming!

Is this real? Am I truly seeing these astonishing things, or am I simply losing my mind…?

Mrs. Gravely has just come in and insists that I set aside my work and get some sleep.

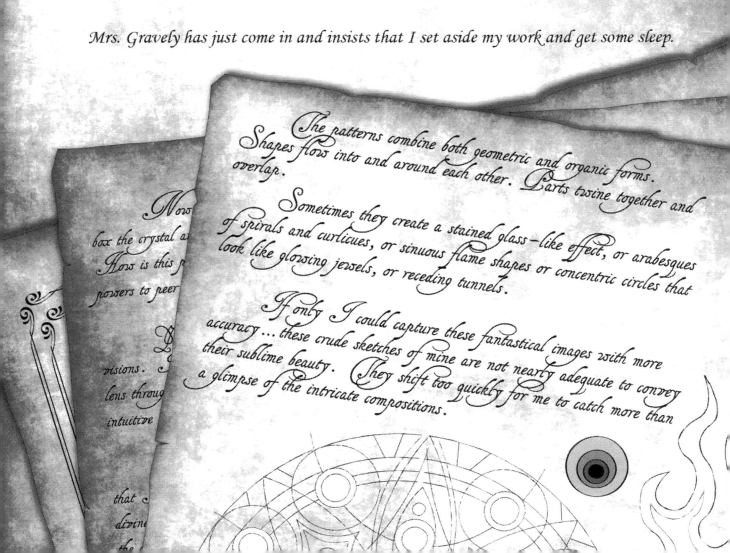

The patterns combine both geometric and organic forms. Shapes flow into and around each other. Parts twine together and overlap.

Sometimes they create a stained glass—like effect, or arabesques of spirals and curlicues, or sinuous flame shapes or concentric circles that look like glowing jewels, or receding tunnels.

If only I could capture these fantastical images with more accuracy … these crude sketches of mine are not nearly adequate to convey their sublime beauty. They shift too quickly for me to catch more than a glimpse of the intricate compositions.

Now
box the crystal a
How is this
powers to peer

visions.
lens throug
intuitive

that
divine

Now I see that the mystifying design printed on the lid of the box the crystal arrived in must be a representation of these mysterious patterns. How is this possible? Was whoever sent me the crystal aware of its powers to peer into this baffling realm?

When it arrived, the crystal was not yet capable of revealing these visions. It was only after I manipulated its shape that the stone became a lens through which to observe this invisible world. Manipulations guided by intuitive dreams...

Or where they, in truth, psychic messages delivered to my mind so that I might discover this amazing phenomenon? Could this be a form of divine inspiration? Like the visions of the Saints, or the ingenious gifts of the ancient Muses?

I feel as if something supernatural is at work here, though I cannot fathom its mechanism or purpose. Have I tapped into some Fundamental aspect of Reality never before witnessed?

It seems too fantastic to be believed!

Though I find myself quite jealous of these discoveries (I am not yet ready to reveal them. I must first find some understanding or context within which to place them before I can present them to the world), I felt that I must have some form of independent confirmation to assure me that I am not simply falling prey to delusions of grandeur or fevered hallucinations. So I casually asked Mrs. Gravely to have a look through the crystal and give me her impressions.

She squinted and moved the crystal about to get her focus (her eyesight has deteriorated in recent years), then smiled brightly.

"My heavens, look at the colors! Quite the spectacle! A new kind of collide-o-scope, is it?"

Her assumption that this was merely some new optical amusement suited my purposes, and I was greatly relieved that she, too, could see the colorful patterns.

"Just so, Mrs. Gravely, though I ask you not to mention it to anyone until I have finished the project. But I needed to be sure that the effect was real and not some mere figment of my imagination."

"Well, I always did think you was a bit touched, Mr. S," she said cheerfully. "But the greatest geniuses always are, ain't they? Fear not, Dear. These old eyes are delighted, and I'm fairly certain I'm not barmy."

So I have ruled out the possibility that the images are hallucinations... but as to whether or not I am a mad genius... I suppose that remains to be seen.

As I continued my observations, I began to experience moments of an odd sensation - the uncanny, hair-raising sense that I was being watched - as if, while I was peering into this bizarre world, so too was I being observed. I chalked it up to being so immersed in the visions beyond the Crystal lens that my awareness of my actual surroundings was minimal, at best.

Perhaps some primal part of my brain was warning me not to divert all of my attentions from my own situation and safety. Of course, I was perfectly safe in my laboratory, so this vague paranoia was unnecessary. Yet it persisted and grew even stronger.

There was such a sense of Presence within the shifting patterns. I cannot adequately describe or explain this feeling, but I found myself searching within the patterns for some suggestion of... Life, I suppose. Indeed, I spied many fleeting compositions that suggested the forms of faces, or animal and floral shapes, and often, the patterns seemed strewn with eye-like motifs that gazed back at me.

Sometimes I caught a glimpse of movements that interrupted the stately and constant pace of transformational shift – almost a fluttering or rippling of the patterns that twisted them into furtive shapes that seemed to surface, and then just as quickly fade back into the prismatic maelstrom.

These flutters became more and more frequent, and the uncomfortable sense of paranoia was replaced with an almost playful purpose. It felt as if someone was teasing me… there was an unmistakable mood of mischievous play; a fantastical game of Hide-and-Seek was afoot, and I became determined to catch the culprit(s) out. I must confess that I became so intent upon this purpose that I began to speak aloud to my elusive quarry. "Come out, then. Don't be shy. Let me have a look at you." …and so on. There was no audible reply, but it did seem as if there was some response – more flutters and twists, accompanied by a sense of affable amusement.

And then, at last, my mysterious playfellow revealed itself – the patterns twisted and parted and a wee face peeked out! It was gone again in a flash, but with more pleading and coaxing, I managed to lure the creature into full view.

Before me was an impossibly beautiful and luminous being of pure color and light. The profundity of my wonderment cannot be overstated. Here was the Presence that I had sensed watching me – there was no doubt that this enchanting creature was alive and possessed of a vibrant consciousness, and that it was aware of me and interacting with me.

Not only had I discovered a new and extraordinary world, but it was inhabited with intelligent life!

I have dubbed the beings "Lumina".

They glow with an inner light, and their forms, while defined, are constantly in flux. Patterns, shapes and colours constantly shift and merge and flow into one another, the complex forms describing their delicate figures.

The colours also shift - gracefully pulsing through the spectrum. The effect is extraordinary! I can sit and gaze at them for hours, rapt with wonder.

They seem to form themselves from the aetheric matter - one moment the patterns will be abstract and seemingly lifeless...and then a Lumina will emerge before me as the patterns warp into a more human-like shape, its eyes shining like jewels. Such riveting eyes! Like glowing gems that seem to gaze deep into my very soul.

They possess a grace that is mesmerizing. Often, their dainty elegance suggests a feminine nature, yet they also, at times, display more masculine features. I am inclined to believe that they are in Truth androgynous creatures. Such gender particularities seem not to apply to them, as they can transform from one to another in a matter of moments. Their appearance is a fluid thing, dictated only by their own wills. The creativity they display is mind-boggling.

Though I cannot hear them, (the Crystal only lets me see into their world) they seem to be able to hear me, or at least sense my presence and respond. After some initial tentativeness, they seem to have accepted my intrusion and even welcome it, appearing before me whenever I gaze through the Crystal. They seem to enjoy my attentions — I sense a benign playfulness and mutual curiosity, and also an undeniable feeling of great intelligence — an Elemental Wisdom that radiates from them.

I am both humbled and exalted by this extraordinary connection.

Color Formula: Rainbow ColorFlow

Try filling each color space with multiple colors that blend into each other. Use Analogous Colors in their natural order to get harmonious blends.

For some vivid contrast, place warm color blends (reds, oranges, yellows) next to or around cool color blends (greens, blues, violets).

ade of pure light and colour.

connected to the aetheric matter

At times, streams of colored patterns fan out around them, forming shapes that resemble wings, giving them the unmistakable appearance of faeries or angels.

Perhaps when the Saints saw visions of angels, it was Lumina they observed – radiant beings with glorious wings, full of divine grace and beauty.

The ancient Pagan religions spoke of Nature Spirits and enigmatic deities who lingered near Holy Wells and other sacred places. Even today, there are those that believe in such things and try to honor and appease them with gifts of food or other offerings.

Could the Lumina be the basis for such myths and visions? Could the stories be true and not merely imaginative fictions or ignorant superstitions?

I have even heard that such ephemeral spirits can be seen in the dreamlike state produced by smoking opium or hashish. Perhaps through an altering of the mental state, this Aetheric Realm I have stumbled upon can be sensed without the aid of an observational device.

The Crystal Prism I have crafted (with seemingly miraculous guidance) may be just one way to access their realm. If they can be contacted through other means - through the ecstasy of fervent prayer or the purity of childhood innocence, or the hypnotic effects of certain plants or even the natural (yet infinitely alien) state of dreaming (as I myself have apparently experienced)… such glimpses of them and communications with them may have inspired many different interpretations through the Ages. Angels, gods, spirits, fluttering pixies and glowing fairy lights.

There are many cultures that speak of other worlds inhabited by supernatural beings, worlds that are separate from our Material Realm, but that can intersect with ours when conditions are right. Legends tell of certain times when the "veil is thin" between worlds, such as twilight and the "Witching Hour", or when astrological signs are in particular alignments.

Some would consider such things unnatural or even demonic, but I sense no malice in the Lumina or their world. They project only beauty and benevolence (and no small amount of gentle humor). They must be a part of the Great Cosmic Order, perhaps acting as divine messengers or serving some other essential purpose in the great scheme of Creation.

Such questions remain a mystery that I am keen to illuminate.

For days on end, I have watched these enchanting creatures, until my eyes grow weary and all is a blur. Poor Mrs. Gravely fears I will harm myself in my rapt obsession. If it were not for her cheerfully bullish insistence that I attend to such trivial matters as eating, sleeping and taking care of myself, perhaps I would indeed have died of fascination.

I find myself frustrated by the limits of my artistic ability, which I once thought was quite considerable, but which now proves wholly inadequate to convey the richness of these Aetherical visions.

I can attain some likeness with my pencils and paints, but the infinitely malleable details and subtle turns of color — the dynamic essence of their forms eludes my efforts to reproduce. Perhaps there is a way to utilize the new photographic processes to capture images of them.

My understanding, however, is that the subject must remain still for long periods of time, which the Lumina are not inclined to do. They are the very essence of endless motion! It is a challenge to which I must apply my mind and find a solution.

In the meantime, I find that the Lumina are teaching me to observe and decipher the nuances of colour with greater depth and insight. The natural order of the chromatic spectrum is luminously evident in their dazzling world. How each colour relates to another, how the interplay between them can create soothing harmonies or vibrant cacophonies of visual delight. These things are often overlooked as we observe our world, but now I find myself noticing them as I go about my days.

I am certain that I appear to have lost my senses, for now the ladies' finery (all adorned with feathers and flowers) seizes my attention in a rather unseemly way. The subtle shades that twist and ripple through the woodgrain of a simple tabletop will distract me from conversation, much to the amusement of my fellows. The rich glow of claret in a glass as it catches the lamplight…I am transfixed, my mind intent upon understanding the play of colours and how they combine to create such brilliant effects.

And the sunsets…my God, the sunsets are now marvelous spectacles to my eyes, wondrous dances of colour that enthrall me more than any gaudy theatrical production.

The Lumina have opened my eyes to new vistas of beauty all around me.

Color Wheel

Fill in the Color Wheel as labeled to familiarize yourself with the natural order of the colors. There is an example on the back cover to guide you.

The Color Wheel can then be used as an invaluable tool for creating color schemes.

There are suggested Color Formulas and color selection methods throughout this book that you can apply to the images, if you wish.

Colour Wheel

Red

"Warm Colors"

Red-Violet

Red Orange

Violet

Orange

Blue-Violet

Yellow Orange

Blue

Yellow

Blue-Green

Yellow-Green

"Cool Colors"

Green

Color Relationships:

Analogous: Colors next to each other on the Color Wheel

Complimentary: Colors directly across from each other on the Color Wheel

Φ Primary Colors   ⊙⊙ Secondary Colors   ◊ Tertiary Colors

The more I get to know them, the more defined the Lumina become. Perhaps my attention inspires them to create more intricate forms. Perhaps they grow more comfortable with my observations. They seem to enjoy showing off, dancing before me for hours, shifting through endless variations of patterns, shapes and colors.

Sometimes the color schemes create distinctive impressions that remind me of certain things; the colors of a forest in autumn, or a field of spring wildflowers. Other times their colors are more subdued and somber, like a misty morning. They flicker like flames, or shimmer as if underwater.

At times, they appear so brilliant that I must squint to discern them. At other times, their colors are dim, almost blending into the darkness, but shot through with brilliant sparks and whispery outlines.

The variety of their appearance is truly infinite!

Today one of the Lumina appeared before me in the guise of a Hindoo goddess - complete with multiple limbs and seated upon a glowing lotus blossom. She conjured swirling flames from the aether, radiating an ineffible sense of serenity and wisdom. I could almost hear the other-worldy sound of sitars playing!

It is extraordinary to think that the ancient sages of India may have communed with these same beings.

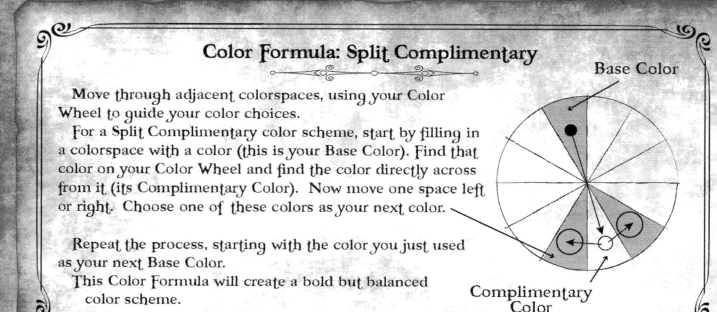

Color Formula: Split Complimentary

Move through adjacent colorspaces, using your Color Wheel to guide your color choices.

For a Split Complimentary color scheme, start by filling in a colorspace with a color (this is your Base Color). Find that color on your Color Wheel and find the color directly across from it (its Complimentary Color). Now move one space left or right. Choose one of these colors as your next color.

Repeat the process, starting with the color you just used as your next Base Color.

This Color Formula will create a bold but balanced color scheme.

Base Color

Complimentary Color

I have been exploring the various photographic methods used to fix an optical image upon a plate. There are a number of different chemical reactions and ...

There ... exposed to th... solution that ...

One ... equipment ... camera obs... perhaps a ... calotype ...

In theory, if I can use the Crystal Prism as a camera lens, the images that I can see through it should be projected ... been ex... amount ... to cre... L... the... reg... ...th of exposure and have ...

After much experimentation and several frustrating setba... I was on the cusp of abandoning my quest to photograph ... Lumina. But in my darkest hour, I once again found inspiration in my dreams.

Last night, a group of industrious Lumina visited my sleeping mind and presented me with marvelous diagrams that showed me how to properly configure my device ... a simple miscalculation when figurin... corrected, would allow ... the plat...

Special Effect: Glowing Stained Glass

Begin by filling in a colorspace with a light base color. Then take a deeper shade of that color (or one of its Analogous Colors, which can be found on either side of it on the Color Wheel) and add a firm application around the edges of that same colorspace. Next, use light pressure and a scribbling stroke to blend the edge shading into the base color. Make sure you leave some of the light base color unshaded – you're going for a bright, glowing center with darker edges.

You can also add some wavery streaks to create a rippled glass effect.

Glowing centers, darker edges

Wavery streaks and ripples

Success!

Now properly configured (thanks to the Lumina's timely and ingenious intervention) my camera functions quite admirably! Though regrettably unable to capture the colors, I have nonetheless been able to produce astonishingly crisp and detailed images.

The shapes and patterns are clearly visible, and I've been experimenting with applying transparent glazes of oil paints to the prints, which, while unable to perfectly mimic the brilliance of the Lumina, create at least some impression of their kaleidoscopic glory.

The images are quite stunning! The Lumina have proven to be very cooperative subjects. I think they quite enjoy having their pictures taken! They seem to perfectly comprehend the process and eagerly appear before the Crystal lens once I have prepared the plate for exposure.

They are naturally adept at presenting beautiful compositions and poses and, to my relief, quite capable of holding still for the exposure. I have noticed that some of them have taken on even more elaborately detailed and refined forms, as if inspired to new heights of creativity.

They are, it seems, quite pleased to display their inventiveness and splendor. Each image is more amazing than the last, and there is no end to their enthusiasm and interest in the project. Most extraordinary!

I must order more photographic supplies.

Special Effect: Radiant Spectrum

To create a radiating rainbow effect on the background pattern, begin with one color for the inner ring of diamond shapes that is visible around the Lumina's chest. Fill in the next ring of diamonds with the next color in the rainbow spectrum. Continue to fill in the concentric rings of diamonds in rainbow color order.

For the space between the diamonds, try leaving it white, or color it black, or try a blend from white — through gray — to black, or from black — through gray — to white.

Initially, the thought of having to hand-tint all of my Luminographs was a bit overwhelming. It seemed a monumental task that would amount to hours and hours of tedious drudgery.

But I have found the opposite to be true!

Each image presents a fresh opportunity to play with color in a way that both sooths and invigorates my senses. There is serenity in the act of flowing the colors into the intricate spaces. Choosing which hues to apply is a combination of intuition and the application of the Natural Laws of Color Theory - Art and Science in perfect harmony!

The Lumina's infinite chromatic variation is an invitation to freely explore color with childlike curiosity and pure joy. There is an element of discovery as the colors find their places, as each piece of the puzzle is locked in and the image is eventually complete. It is a moment of sublime transformation – from mere dabs of pigment into a harmonious Whole.

It is visual alchemy, chromatic magic, tapping deep into the primal flow of Pure Creation.

Time seems to stand still, and all else fades away when I engage in this activity. It is a state of blissful focus and relaxation. At times it can be challenging – finding the precise shade to choose - but if I surrender myself to the process, explore the possibilities and listen to the colors – the perfect choice always comes to me eventually.

At times I feel as if the Lumina are guiding me, whispering in my ear, making suggestions or offering inspiration. We are dancing together, spinning through pure color, creating brilliant choreographies of rhythm and hue. The colors are like music and motion and mood, playing upon the eye and the heart and the mind.

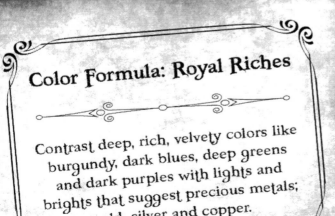

Color Formula: Royal Riches

Contrast deep, rich, velvety colors like burgundy, dark blues, deep greens and dark purples with lights and brights that suggest precious metals; gold, silver and copper.

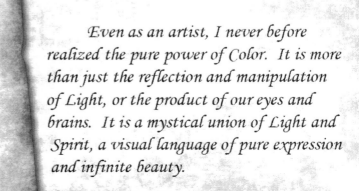

Even as an artist, I never before realized the pure power of Color. It is more than just the reflection and manipulation of Light, or the product of our eyes and brains. It is a mystical union of Light and Spirit, a visual language of pure expression and infinite beauty.

The Lumina are masters not only of their own forms, but of the aetheric matter that surrounds them. I suspect they are one and the same — the Lumina are the aether itself, somehow imbued with consciousness and intent, just as all Living Things are made of matter, yet possess the mysterious volition of Life.

They manipulate the abstract patterns into fabulous compositions of color and form; spills of twinkling stars, swirling mandalas and radiant sunbursts, like multicolored fireworks. They are truly consummate artists, every move a graceful act of creation that ripples through the aether, giving it form and presence.

I can't help but wonde[r ...] [...] Lumina are somehow connected to [the] very process of Creation [...] [man]ipulation of the [...]ther is akin to our own in[...] [...]reate.

They take the raw [...] something more than just [...] combining elements into [...]

Their invent[...]

Every aspect of t[...] [...] is ours.

Color Formula: Rhapsody in Blues

Fill in most of the colorspaces with various shades of Blue, Blue-Green and Blue-Violet. Make sure to include both lights (ex: Light Aqua) and darks (ex: Ultramarine) to create visual interest. Try placing Analogous Colors next to each other in order to create a spectrum shift effect: Blue Green – to – Blue – to – Blue-Violet.
Try layering colors over one another to create even more variety.
Accent the Blues with some Cool Grays and a few areas of pale, warm shades like Cream, Light Golden Yellow and Peach.

One of the Lumina I observed today presented itself in the softest hues that glowed with an ethereal luminescence. Instead of the bright, vivid colors they usually display, this one had a ghostly, ephemeral countenance, like a phantom or apparition.

The colors were sublimely subtle — pale, faded shades of every color of the spectrum so translucent and delicate that a pure, radiant white light shined through them. The effect was akin to the glow of gaslight through softly tinted, frosted glass.

It reminded me of scientist-turned-mystic Swedenborg's notions of the spirit world. He proposed that after death, human Souls become either angelic or demonic spirits, depending on the virtue of the deeds they performed during their lives.

According to his writings, these angelic spirits can communicate with living humans through dreams and visions, and influence us with their divine auras.

Could this be the True Nature of the Lumina? Could the angels Swedenborg claimed to have communicated with be the same beings I now observe through my Crystal Prism?

Are they the souls of the departed, now filled with Divine Grace? Could this Aetheric Realm in fact be Heaven itself?

And could sightings of ghosts and spirits also be attributed to the Lumina?

They are so mysterious and malleable that they can be interpreted in an infinite variety of ways.

Color Formula: Ethereal Apparition

To create a ghostly, ethereal effect, limit your palette to pale, faded colors and light grays and leave some white showing through as your lightest areas.

Using a very light touch, blend the pastel colors into the white so you get a smooth transition.

Build up some slightly deeper shades in a few areas with soft layers.

Try for a softly glowing effect.

Color Formula: Lumina's Choice

Gather all of your bright, vivid colors, discarding neutrals and pastels, and lay them out before you. Close your eyes and let the Lumina choose a color. Scan the image until you find the perfect place for it to go.

Sometimes there may be multiple colorspaces that call to you. Listen to your intuition — the Lumina are whispering to you!

After you use a color, move it to a "discard pile".

Continue to allow the Lumina to guide your color choices until you have used each color in your original selection, then start the whole process over again from the beginning, until the image is complete.

Lumina manipulating the Aether – detail

I have discovered that darkness is not, in fact, necessary to see the images through the Crystal Prism. While the contrast of the darkness does make Lumina's aetheric glow all the brighter, I've found that I can still discern them reasonably well in subdued light. Perhaps my eyes have grown more adept at detecting the aetheric energies.

This discovery has lead me to even more fascinating observations.

In the dim light, I can see both the Lumina and the material world around me, and, to my astonishment, I found that they are not mutually exclusive domains!

The Lumina interact with our world, though much of their activity is still mysterious to me.

As I sweep the Crystal's gaze around the laboratory, I see how the aether flows around and through the furnishings and other solid objects. When the Lumina are intent upon something, the aether seems to coalesce around it, echoing the material shapes in aetheric patterns. It is as if the Lumina are somehow attaching the aetheric energy to things. It is difficult to describe.

They seem to cluster around certain things — my painting area is of particular fascination for them. I often see them fluttering around my palette, or the jars of pigments. My bookshelves are another favorite haunt.

One day, Mrs. Gravely brought in a vase of flowers she'd cut from the garden (as usual, nattering amiably about how I am spending far too much time in my lab and need to get some fresh air or I will surely expire), and the Lumina flocked to the colorful arrangement and spun wondrous aetheric visions around it.

Perhaps it is color itself that attracts them...?

Color Formula: Green Goddess

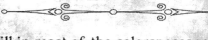

Fill in most of the colorspaces with various shades of Green, Blue-Green and Yellow-Green. Make sure to include both lights and darks to create visual interest. Try placing Analogous Colors next to each other in order to create a spectrum shift effect: Yellow-Green —to - Green —to — Blue Green.

Try layering colors over one another to create even more variety.

Create some dramatic accents with contrasting shades of Orange, Yellow, Gold, Peach and Pink.

On a whim, I ventured outside at twilight with my Crystal Prism in hand. To my delight, in the gloaming, a spectacular wonderland was revealed to me. Lumina were everywhere – clustered around every bud and blossom! Though the fleeing light left the garden rather flat and colorless to my naked eyes, every flower they touched became a glowing, kaleidoscopic burst of aetheric color within the world beyond the Crystal's lens.

They were busily blessing each petal with pulsing luminescence, until the garden was a splendid spectacle of fairy lights. Peering closer, I saw that some of the Lumina were even taking on the forms of the flowers themselves, sprouting shapes that suggested gay petals and leaves. How lovely they are!

Perhaps they are absorbing something from the colors of our world, feeding on the chromatic energy somehow, yet enhancing it at the same time…?

Even when I lowered the Crystal and surveyed the darkening garden, the colors now seemed somehow fresher and lovelier to my eyes. One rose in particular caught my attention. Through the Crystal, I saw several Lumina tending to it, weaving aetheric traceries along its sensuous curves and folds. They seemed to beckon, inviting me to drink in its loveliness. It was perfect – at the peak of its glory, soon to fade.

I was seized with the notion to pluck it. I knew who else would appreciate its splendor. As the last of the evening's light faded into darkness, I went in and found Mrs. Gravely working diligently in the kitchen, preparing supper. She was surprised to see me there and even more surprised when I presented her with the perfect rose.

"I may not express it often enough, Mrs. Gravely", said I, "but I am most grateful for your care and companionship and constant good cheer. Thank you for keeping me alive and in good health and fretting over me so. I would be lost without you."

She blushed furiously and waved me off, but as she gazed at the rose, I saw tears glistening in her merry eyes, and I could sense the Lumina around us - invisible, but radiating their delight.

I have devised an apparatus that will allow me to gaze through the Crystal Prism while leaving my hands free. It was becoming tedious to have to hold the lens up to my eye whenever I wanted a look through it.

My "Prismascope" is based upon a pair of spectacles, but modified to my specific purposes. In order to position the lens correctly before my eye while blocking out extraneous light, I built a setting for the Crystal Prism within an adjustable oculus on the right side of the frame (before my stronger eye), while covering the left side with a leather patch and surrounding the whole with leather pieces formed to fit the contours of my face.

Both eyepieces are hinged to allow me to turn them up out of the way if I wish an unobstructed view. I have also included a smoked glass lens that quite admirably mimics the effect of dim twilight, allowing me to see both the Material and Aetheric Realms at once, even in full daylight!

It may be a curious looking device, but it has already proven itself an essential instrument to advance my studies.

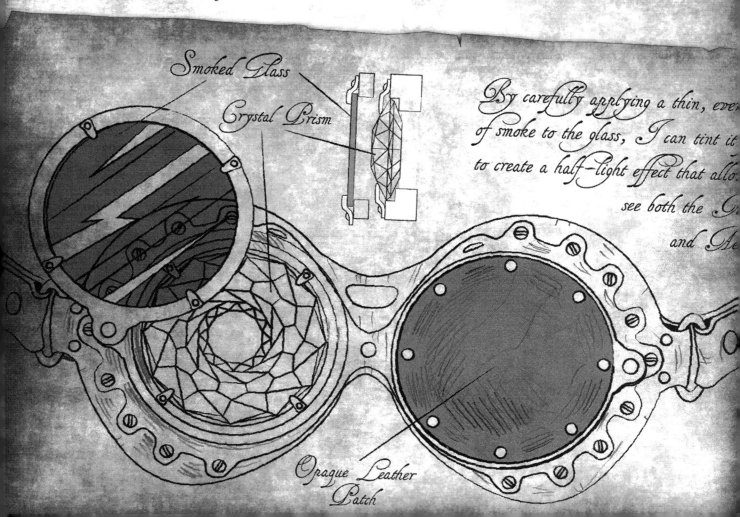

Smoked Glass

Crystal Prism

By carefully applying a thin, even
of smoke to the glass, I can tint it
to create a half-light effect that allo
see both the G
and Ae

Opaque Leather
Patch

The Lumia inspire me so! Their presence is a soothing balm to my racing mind, so bursting with questions and ideas.

I have noticed a distinctive clarity of thought that allows me to make intuitive connections and pursue the solutions to problems with greater dexterity and insight than ever before.

I suspect that my interaction with the Aetheric Realm has somehow influenced my flexibility of mind, expanding my capability to grasp and elucidate complex thoughts and ideas.

Perhaps the aether is not just a conduit for Light and Color, but for the free flow of Thoughts and Ideas as well!

Watching the endlessly changing, infinitely complex, yet perfectly balanced and harmonious patterns has a mesmerizing effect almost akin to a trance, but retaining a full sense of awareness.

This mental state seems to facilitate the generation of novel concepts and heightened creativity. It is as if my brain's potential for intuitive insight has been increased!

I wonder if the Great Geniuses of the past felt this kind of sublime inspiration. I wonder if the Lumina have always been secret allies of Humankind – their invisible presence an unacknowledged but essential part of our History and Progress.

Perhaps the aether allows them to touch our minds in subtle, yet powerful ways - nurturing our development, guiding us to ever greater abilities and acheivements.

As I watch the Lumina shift through their endless transformations, I am struck by how much just a change in their color palette can dramatically alter the general impression their appearance creates.

For example, a Lumina appeared before me today in the guise of an old, bearded man. Its beard was made of spiraling swirls, and its eyes twinkled with wisdom and compassion,

As the colors slowly changed, he became a green and earthy forest spirit - the very personification of the ancient, primal beauty of Nature.

Then the colors deepened into rich jewel tones accented with the gleam of precious metals, creating the impression of a powerful wizard or emperor.

When vivid shades of red and green and silver arose, it seemed the very likeness of jolly Father Christmas himself!

It is apparent that we have many complex mental associations with particular combinations of colors that develop throughout our lives. Some of these are archetypes that have surely been a part of our collective human experience for millennia; others are products of our more modern culture and personal experiences.

Certain color schemes remind us of these concepts, influencing us on a deep level, stirring emotions and conveying complicated ideas - just as the melodic language of music can conjure vivid mental fantasies. The greatest artists and composers know this, and apply their mastery of these non-verbal languages to speak to us on a level that goes deeper than mere intellect.

I believe the Lumina communicate with us on this deep, spiritual level - activating our own imaginations with their innate creative powers.

I have prepared my manuscript and presentation for my meeting with the British Association for the Advancement of Science. I travel tomorrow to London, where I shall reveal my discoveries to the most celebrated men of science still living. I am quite nervous. I am confident in my work, but the prospect of this momentous occasion and what it could mean for me, my career, the world...

I fear they will dismiss my claims as flimflammery or the ravings of a madman, and the Luminographs as mere optical trickery. But when they see what the Crystal Prism reveals to their very own eyes, they cannot possibly doubt the reality, wonder and sceintific importance of these incredible discoveries!

Color Formula: Purple Passion

Fill in most of the colorspaces with various shades and blends of Violets, Blue-Violets, Pinks, Red-Violets (such as Magenta or Fuschia) and cool Reds. Avoid warm, Orange-Reds.

Try placing Analogous Colors next to each other in order to create a spectrum shift effect: Blue-Violet - to - Violet - to - Pink.

Create some dramatic accents in a few places with contrasting shades of Greens, Yellow-Greens and Blue-Greens.

Color Formula: Firestarter

Fill in most of the colorspaces with various shades and blends of Yellows, Oranges and Reds.

Try placing Analogous Colors next to each other in order to create a spectrum shift effect: Yellow - to - Orange - to - Red.

Create some dramatic accents with contrasting shades of Blue, Purple and Magenta.
Avoid any shades of Green.

It's broken. The Prism is cracked in two.

Just as I was about to demonstrate my Prismascope, my nervous fingers fumbled and it slipped from my grasp. It seemed to tumble in slow-motion as my heart dropped into my stomach. It landed with a terrible, crystalline clink. When I examined the Crystal, I saw the crack split down the middle – like a gleaming, glaring wound.

With my last shred of Hope, I gazed through it and found that whatever magic my careful sculpting had facilitated was gone. There were no visions to be seen, no dancing colors or luminous spirits. Merely a gaudy trinket, cracked in two, showing only a fractured and distorted view of our mundane reality.

I felt the color drain from my face. It seemed my very soul faded and bleached out as I realized that I would not be able to share my discoveries after all.

All I had now was my research and writings, my sketches and illustrations and the Luminographs...all of them amounting to dubious fancy without the indisputable proof now broken and useless in my hands.

The fellows were very nice about it. Quite polite. They said I could return at any time when I had succeeded in securing the evidence they required for consideration.

I tried not to notice the looks they gave each other, those secret little knowing glances that covertly communicated their silent judgment of me and my work – rubbish, madness, fraud, inadequacy.

I am humiliated. All the work of these past, extraordinary months is ruined.

Color Formula: Nature Spirit

Play with your earthy, organic colors to create the impression of an ancient Nature Spirit.

Explore your greens, golds, browns, grays and neutrals. Imagine the colors of a forest - leafy foliage, rich soil, reddish clay, stones streaked with various minerals, fallen leaves, dappled sunlight.

Accent these earthy shades with a few brighter colors found in nature. Imagine fruits, wildflowers, colorful mushrooms, autumn leaves and butterflies.

As I made my way home from London, I was inconsolable. Not only had my presentation been an utter disaster, I was now cut off from the Aetheric Realm. With the Crystal broken, I could no longer see into that mesmerizing world. I could not see my precious Lumina.

Gazing out at the countryside passing by my carriage, the world looked gray and lifeless. All the colors had fled.

After several days of melancholic despair spent mostly abed in a pitiful state, Mrs. Gravely finally insisted that I pull myself together and carry on. She fortified me with some strong Earl Grey, then practically shoved me out the door and into the garden.

I steeled myself as I entered this once-joyous place, expecting it to feel empty and somber without the sight of Lumina flitting about. But to my surprise, it was not so: the foliage and blossoms were still merry and vivid and I felt my spirits rise despite myself.

Though I could no longer see the Lumina with my eyes, I could still feel their presence. I could, if I closed my eyes and quieted my mind, still sense the subtle current of aetheric energy flowing around me.

As I wandered through the lush riot of colorful blooms, I realized that I had not lost my connection with the Lumina after all. They were still with me, radiating their infinite love and gentle humor, still touching my Soul with their numinous serenity and endless creativity.

Perhaps the Lumina are not meant to be studied and codified. Perhaps their Mystery is an essential part of their power to fascinate and inspire us.

Like the Muses of old, they exert their subtle influence in ways that the Human Mind cannot fathom, charging our dreams with infinite possibilities, guiding our thoughts from chaos to order, infusing our minds with creative inspiration and spiritual encouragement.

To reduce them to mundane objects to be examined, measured and catalogued now seems a ludicrous notion to me. One cannot test and dissect the Aetheric Realm as we can the Material World. We can only experience it and marvel at its ineffable splendor.

Though my Crystal Prism window into their world remains closed to me, I can still feel the Lumina's presence and influence. They remind me to take the time to watch the magical metamorphosis of Day into Night, to revel in the delicate beauty and breathtaking grandeur of the Natural World, to allow my mind to explore and play and wander along paths that lead me to new and intriguing discoveries.

And sometimes - out of the corner of my eye – peeking out from within the velvet petals of a perfect bloom, or dancing in the shiver of leaves in the breeze...

...Just for a moment, I think I see them - smiling at me with their luminous eyes, spinning their colorful magic - then once again disappearing into the aether.

Ed. Note: Though my own research on these materials has revealed little to add, it's possible that more evidence of Smythe's work and of the reality of the Lumina may exist, somewhere out there. If you come across anything, please let me know!

A Few Words From The Artist...

Inspiration

The impetus for this book was threefold:
1.   I wanted to combine the meditative, freestyle flow of abstract mandalas with figurative art in a way that would result in beautiful finished pieces.
2.   I have always wanted to create a work of fiction that made fantasy seem like reality. My favorite books as a kid, the ones that really lit my imagination and stoked the fire, approached fantasy as if it were real. I knew they were fiction, of course…but the conceit gave me permission to believe, even if for only a moment, that maybe there was some secret, magical reality that lay hidden behind our mundane world, waiting to be uncovered and explored by those who have the imagination and faith to seek it out.
3.   I wanted to make a coloring book that was more than just a collection of images. I wanted to create an experience that would spark the imagination as well as encourage creative color play.

I had these strange and beautiful images of "mandala fairies" that danced through my mind, begging to be manifested on paper and filled with color, and eventually, a fictional context for them came to me. These images seemed to flow through me with such ease and bliss …perhaps the Lumina *are* real…whispering to me in my dreams and artistic visions, so they could go out into the world and connect with all of you!

Research

The Victorian Age was one of great change, excitement and drama. The Western World experienced unparalleled revolutions in cultural, spiritual and technological paradigms. I must admit that I am quite glad I did not live through those times for a number of reasons, but it is a period of history I find fascinating.

Here are some of the subjects I explored while researching for this book that I found to be particularly interesting. I encourage you to explore them as well. Most of them have entries on Wikipedia.com to get you started.

(cont.)

History of Photography
Sir Isaac Newton's work with Light and Color
Goethe's works on Light and Color
David Brewster's inventions
Emmanuel Swedenborg's mystical writings
Fairy lore
Viking Sunstones
The Luminiferous Aether

ColorFlow

This book features an art style I've been developing that I think of as "ColorFlow". This involves a lot of graceful shapes that wrap around each other, entwine together, overlap and offer opportunities to create color patterns. Complex shapes often wander into unexpected places.

You need a certain amount of focus as you explore each shape with your coloring tip, following its path as it flows around adjacent colorspaces, or underneath overlapping shapes. This creates a sense of exploration and discovery that I think adds to the coloring experience. I find that this level of focus and flow creates a wonderful, meditative state of mind.

The mandala-like quality of the imagery allows you to play freely with pure color. I've never had so much fun coloring than I've had test coloring these images. :)

Color Formulas and Special Effects

I have included several "Color Formulas" and "Special Effects" suggestions you can try, if you need inspiration or want to challenge yourself. They are completely optional, and can be applied to any image, not just the ones they are across from.

Some of them require consulting a Color Wheel. There is one included in this book for you to fill in, and a colored sample on the back cover as a guide.

Coloring Page Gallery

Visit my website: www.GypsyMystery.com to see a collection of colored images from this book, as well as my other books.

I encourage you to share your colored pages online, but ask that you please include my name and the title of the book in your posts.

About the Artist

I've been compelled to draw and create since I could hold a crayon, and have spent the first half of my life teaching myself how to develop that natural talent. I have worked as a professional artist and illustrator since my teens, exploring many genres and creative industries.

In 2011, my amazing husband and I combined his building skills and my artistic flair to create Calliope The Wonder Wagon - a gypsy-style camper trailer and mobile work of art. Find out more about Calliope on my website: www.GypsyMystery.com.

My quest to infuse this collaborative project with meaning led me to explore the fascinating world of symbolic imagery. This new direction also took me on a journey into the mystical and sacred realms, exploring spiritual traditions from around the world. These ideas sparked many art pieces intended to not only please the eye, but to inspire mindfulness, reverence and celebration.

In 2014, I began exploring jewelry making and accessory design. My handmade fantasy fashion accessories can be found on my Etsy shop: https://www.etsy.com/shop/cristinamcallister

In 2015, I discovered coloring books for adults, and a whole new world of possibilties opened up to me. I hope to continue to explore this art form and create more fun and beautiful interactive art that we can collaborate on together.

If you enjoyed this book, please take a few moments to post a review on the Amazon.com listing page. These reviews really do make a huge difference for self-publishers and artists. Your feedback and support are invaluable!

Thanks for Coloring with me!

Gypsy Mystery Arts

Made in the USA
San Bernardino, CA
12 July 2016